Turnabout

A MUSICAL VERSION
OF THE BOOK OF ESTHER

Book, Music, and Lyrics
by Ken Easton and Jack Sharkey

SAMUEL FRENCH, INC.

25 WEST 45TH STREET   NEW YORK 10036
7623 SUNSET BOULEVARD   HOLLYWOOD 90046
LONDON   *TORONTO*

...ASTON AND JACK SHARKEY

...RVED

NOTE ON MUSIC: Choral parts are available for purchase at
$2.00 per copy, plus post. The royalty fee for the use of this music,
which is in addition to royalty on the play itself, is $5.00 for each
performance. The music royalty must be paid at the time of ordering
the choral parts.

PRINTED IN U. S. A.

No changes shall be made in the play for the purpose of
your production unless authorized in writing.

ISBN 0 573 62527 1

CAST OF CHARACTERS

ESTHER, obedient niece of
MORDECHAI, a deeply religious Jew
KING, of The Persian Empire
HAMAN, a scheming Persian noble
ZARES, the wife of Haman
MAJOR-DOMO, of the Royal Palace
BAGATHAN ⎫
THARES ⎭ treasonous eunuchs
MISS ABYSSINIA ⎫
MISS SARDINIA
MISS THRACE
MISS PHRYGIA
MISS UR
MISS MACEDONIA
MISS LACONIA
MISS SUDAN
MISS SUMERIA ⎬ beauty contestants
MISS CRETE
MISS JORDAN
MISS CARTHAGE
MISS CYPRUS
MISS CORINTH
MISS CADIZ
MISS CHALDEA ⎭
Plus GUARDS, COURTIERS, TOWNSPEOPLE, SERVANTS,
HANDMAIDENS, NOBLES, EUNUCHS, etc.

(Casting Note: The 16 beauty contestants, after their
two musical numbers, can of course fill in as handmaidens, townswomen, courtiers' wives, and so forth.)

3

TIME: Way, way back, about 1000 B.C.

PLACE: The Royal Palace in Susan, capital city of the Persian Empire—a vast territory encompassing the Mediterranean Countries, Northern Africa, Arabia and India.

MUSICAL NUMBERS

"WHAT'LL WE CALL THE KING?" . *Townspeople*

"WE'RE GONNA HAVE A PARTY!" . *Townspeople*

"BEAUTY PAGEANT" .... *Major-Domo*

"ESTHER!" .... *King, Esther & Chorus*

"SHE'S SO LOVELY!" .... *Beauty Contestants*

"TWO EUNUCHS ARE PLOTTING" .. *Mordechai, Esther, King*

"WHY, WHY, MORDECHAI?" .. *Haman & Zares*

"I'D GIVE HIM GOLD" .... *Haman*

" 'TIS DEATH" .... *Esther & Handmaidens*

"TANGO FOR A TWO-TIMER" .... *Haman, Mordechai, Esther, King*

"I SAID I'M SORRY" ...... *Haman, Esther, King*

"ESTHER!" (Reprise) .... *Everybody but Haman & Zares*

5

PRONUNCIATION GUIDE FOR
ANCIENT NAMES

Susan: SOO-sahn

Xerxes: ZURK-seez

Artaxerxes: ar-tax-URK-seez

Ahasuerus: ah-ha-SOO-er-us

Vashti: VAHSH-tee

Haman: HAY-mun

Zares: ZAY-reez

Bagathan: buh-GAYTH-un

Thares: THAY-reez

Phrygia: FRIDGE-ee-uh

Sumeria: soo-MAIR-ee-uh

Chaldea: CHAL-dee-uh

Mordechai: MOR-duh-kye

Turnabout

*Curtain rises on Throne Room of the Palace: Two
thrones side by side on a dais upstage center,
accesses to the room at extreme left and right.
Decor as simple or lavish as the budget dictates,
and the same goes for the costumes, which should
be of the tunic/robe/burnoose variety. Stage is
untenanted at curtain-rise, and then* MORDECHAI,
*a middle-aged man of pleasant aspect, strolls in
and addresses us.*

MORDECHAI. Hello, there. My name is Mordechai,
and—as one of the people involved in the story you're
about to see—I thought I might just sort of act as
your guide through the coming events. (TOWNSPEOPLE
start wandering onstage.) About three thousand years
ago, in a city called Susan, there lived a very great
king. By today's standards, he was somewhat barbaric
and cruel—but for those days, he was a real pussy-
cat. His people liked him, and—in his somewhat lofty
way—he liked them too. As our story begins, the word
has gone out that the king has a rather important an-
nouncement to make, so his people have shown up at
the royal palace to find out what it is—and to discuss
among themselves a peculiar problem of the times, a
problem based upon the fact that communications
were poor, and that multiple languages abounded, and
that very few of the people could read, anyhow, even
if there had been newspapers—of which, of course,
there weren't any. . . .

7

(*MUSIC INTROS, and* Townspeople *move downstage
while* Mordechai *exits, and then they begin to
sing, both to us and to one another:*)

Townspeople.
We would like to express our views on
Daily life in the town of Susan
In the reign of our beloved king.

We are stuck with a tough dilemma:
When the king or his royal emi—
Ssary shows up, then our hands we wring.

There is not a doubt,
If the truth came out,
Our problem might appall him.
For we all have found,
When the king's around,
We don't know what to call him!

What'll we call the king?
What do you call a man who's known by
Practic'ly anything you could proclaim?

What'll we call the king?
We could endanger all we own by
Making the rafters ring with the wrong name!
    Men.
Sometimes he's known as Xerxes . . .
    Women.
But also Artaxerxes . . .
    Man.
And sometimes Ahasuerus . . .
    All.
What would you do if you were us?

What'll we call the king?
Here we all stand while time has flown by,
Wishing that we could sing his name with glee . . .
   MEN.
On needles and pins—
   WOMEN.
To save our skins—
   ALL.
We'll say, "Your majesty" . . .
   MAN.
'Cause—
   ALL.
The only thing
We can call the king
Is:
Very carefully!

(MAJOR-DOMO *enters, and* TOWNSPEOPLE *peel back into two respectful groups, exposing throne area.*)

MAJOR-DOMO. Make way for the king! Make way for the ruler of the endless Persian Empire that does extend from Ethiopia even unto the eastern mountains of India. Bend your knees as the king approaches his royal throne! (TOWNSPEOPLE *drop to one knee as* KING *enters, strolling slowly and regally, followed by* HAMAN, ZARES, BARATHAN, THARES, *and assorted* COURTIERS *and* NOBLES, *during:*) All hail to Xerxes the First, the Lion King, Artaxerxes, the Eye of Man, Ahasuerus, the Mighty, the Splendid, the Beloved, etcetera, etcetera, etcetera!

(MAJOR-DOMO, HAMAN, ZARES, BAGATHAN, THARES, COURTIERS *and* NOBLES *all bow low, and back slightly away as* KING *sits on larger of two thrones; then, as they straighten:*)

KING. I suppose you're all wondering why I've called you here today . . . ?

HAMAN. It did cross my mind, sire.

ZARES. Mine, too.

KING. It has come to my attention that there is no war in my empire—that there is no famine—very little poverty—reasonably low taxes—lots of nice weather—no particular pestilence—fish are jumpin' and the cotton is high. Am I correct—? (ALL *ad-lib quickly* "*You bet!*", "*Right on!*", "*Yessiree!*" *etc.*) In such circumstance, it seems to me that we should celebrate our good fortune. Do you not agree? (ALL *ad-lib similarly, again.*) Therefore, beginning this very night, I have decided to have a small party . . .

NOBLES. For the nobles?

COURTIERS. For the courtiers?

TOWNSPEOPLE. For the people?

HAMAN. For *me*—? (ZARES *elbows him, and he appends hastily:*) and my gal?

KING. The answer to each of your questions is—yes!

MAJOR-DOMO. You mean, sire—*everybody* is invited?

KING. Everybody over whom the flag of the Persian Empire flies.

HAMAN. That's everybody, all right!

KING. And the party shall last until Harvest Day.

MAJOR-DOMO. Harvest Day, your majesty? Why—that's not until autumn—and we are barely into spring!

KING. I know you're disappointed it's so short—but we can't spend *all* the year whooping it up, can we?

MAJOR-DOMO. No, sire.

HAMAN. Of course not.

ZARES. Naturally.

KING. (*Rises.*) Well, I'm going to get on my fancy clothes. See you all at dinner! (KING *and same entourage that followed him on will all exit,* MAJOR-DOMO *departing last, during:*)

TOWNSPEOPLE. Wowee!

WOMEN. Did you hear that?!

MEN. A royal party lasting all spring and summer long!

WOMAN. And I haven't got a thing to wear!

ALL. (*Sing.*)

We're gonna have a party! A really royal party!
A party that will startle and amaze!
The check we'll never have to grab:
The king is picking up the tab!
It's gonna run one-hundred-eighty days!

We're gonna have a party! A really royal party!
Six months of making whoopee and good cheer!
We'll get our kicks for twenty-six
Long weeks, so bring a lot of mix,
And canapes enough for half a year!

Knife, fork and spoon will croon a tune
And sing right through the coda!

MEN.
And at each feast—

WOMEN.
Last but not least—

ALL.
Bicarbonate of soda!
We're gonna have a party! A really royal party!

WOMAN.
Just think of all the weight we're gonna gain!

ALL.
We're surely gonna stretch our skin,

But folks are very sure that in
The reign of our good king we'll feel no pain . . .
And that is why we're singing in the reign!

(*MUSIC CONTINUES, and* TOWNSPEOPLE *dance, and*
    MORDECHAI *re-enters, watching them; then, as
    they reach a pause in the dance, he turns to us,
    and:*)

MORDECHAI. It was really a lot of fun, but we
needn't go into the details here. Let's move ahead in
our story to a point one-hundred-seventy-three days
later . . .

(TOWNSPEOPLE, *now sagging and subdued, come for-
    ward to sing again, and* MORDECHAI *exits quietly,
    during:*)

ALL.
We're weary of the party, this never-ending party!
There's nothing quite so glassy as our gaze . . .
With headaches all our heads are cleft!
Thank heaven there's just one week left!
We hope the king does not miscount the days!

We're weary of the party, this never-ending party!
We'd love to stop and nevermore resume!
We're going mad from lack of sleep,
And if just one more plate we heap,
We're gonna wind up in a rubber room!
    MEN.
And now, we find, the way we've dined—
    WOMEN.
While topping off with pie, yet!

MEN.

For one whole generation, then—

ALL.

We'll all be on a diet!

MEN.

We're weary of the party!

WOMEN.

Oh, please call off the party!

WOMAN.

We should have guessed the finish at the start!

MAN.

Though no one's an enthusiast—

WOMAN # 2.

A royal mandate holds us fast—

MAN # 2.

But if the king would bid us to depart . . .

ALL.

We'd bless his royal party-pooping heart!

(TOWNSPEOPLE *sag and shuffle glumly off, as* MOR-
DECHAI *re-enters;* KING *and entourage will re-
enter during his next speech, and take their former
places.*)

MORDECHAI. As people are so slow to learn, you *can*
get too much of a good thing! In fact, one of the
earliest persons to poop out during the hectic and endless celebration was Queen Vashti, who was never
much of a gadabout to begin with. So naturally, she
was not anywhere around, when . . . (*He moves into
scene, at far end of assembled entourage, on:*)

KING. I'm awfully tired of sitting on this throne just
watching the fun.

HAMAN. Why not join in the dancing, then, sire?

KING. That's easy for *you* to say, Haman. You have

your faithful wife Zares right beside you, all the time! But I'm not much for solo dancing.

MAJOR-DOMO. And pity 'tis that only a queen may dance with your royal majesty, yet Queen Vashti seldom graces celebratory events with her presence.

ZARES. (*To* HAMAN.) Husband—bid him send for her!

HAMAN. I can't do that! The king takes orders from nobody!

ZARES. If you don't, he's going to turn sour on the whole party, and when a king turns sour, heads start to roll, and your head is the nearest to the throne!

HAMAN. You talked me into it! (*To* KING.) Sire, rather than languish alone on the throne, shall you not be more pleasantly occupied if you do send for your wife to join you? After all, by the royal rules, she may not approach you until you *do* send for her. Perhaps she is merely awaiting your call—?

KING. You are right, Haman! I *did* forget! Major-Domo—summon to me at once my queen, the beauteous Vashti!

MAJOR-DOMO. You there! You two eunuchs! (BAGATHAN *and* THARES *hurry forward.*) Hasten apace to the royal harem, and thence bring forth unto us the queen herself! (*They exit immediately, and he turns back to the* KING.) They'll be quick, sire. The nice thing about being eunuchs is that they can walk into the harem without knocking. (*They re-enter immediately, and rush to* MAJOR-DOMO, *who reacts:*) What, back so soon, and as yet unaccompanied by the queen?

BAGATHAN. "As yet" doesn't say it.

THARES. "Not at all" is more like it.

KING. You have dared to return with your mission unaccomplished?!

BAGATHAN. Oh, sire, we did do *our* part!

THARES. We went—

BAGATHAN. We entered—

THARES. We asked—

BAGATHAN. She answered—

THARES. We left—

BAGATHAN. And here we are!

KING. Fools! This much can I see for myself! Where is Queen Vashti!?

BAGATHAN. Welllll—

THARES. It's like this—

KING. Tempt not my wrath by hesitation! What did the queen say?

BAGATHAN. She's very tired—

THARES. Her head aches—

BAGATHAN. Her feet hurt—

THARES. And she just washed her hair—

BAGATHAN. So therefore—

THARES. She's not coming!

KING. What?

MAJOR-DOMO. Not?

BAGATHAN and THARES. Coming.

KING. This is an outrage! Guards, take these two eunuchs hence, and have them flogged!

BAGATHAN. Who?

THARES. Us?

BOTH. It's not *our* fault!

KING. And two extra lashes for backtalk!

BAGATHAN. (*A mutter, as* GUARDS *lead them out.*) Sorehead!

THARES. You can say that again!

KING. (*When they are gone.*) Oh, this is an unpardonable insult! Heads shall roll for this! Starting with . . . (*Looks about, comes almost nose-to-nose with* HAMAN.)

ZARES. (*Close behind* HAMAN, *urges:*) Quick, you idiot, say something!

HAMAN. Hey! You know what? I just got a terrific idea!

KING. What is it?

HAMAN. (*To* ZARES.) What is it?

ZARES. Have him pick a *new* queen!

HAMAN. Sire! Why don't you pick yourself a *new* queen?!

KING. A new queen? Say—that's not a bad idea—all the best-looking maidens in my far-flung empire are here for the party—I could have my pick of any of them!

HAMAN. Right! And I'll take charge of the entire thing, too, so you don't have to worry your royal head about details, okay?

KING. You've got a deal, Haman! And if it works out—well—I owe you a favor!

HAMAN. Oh boy! (*To* MAJOR-DOMO:) You heard what the king said! Get the show on the road!

MAJOR-DOMO. Okay-okay, stop pushing! (*Starts for exit, but is drawn aside by* MORDECHAI.) What do *you* want?

MORDECHAI. Do I understand it that *any* maiden in the empire is eligible? See, I have this daughter—at least, she's my adopted daughter—she was my niece, but her parents died, and—

MAJOR-DOMO. Look, I've got my own troubles. If she's not bad to look at, and she's a maiden eligible for marriage—bring the kid around. By the way—what's her name?

MORDECHAI. *Esther!* Excuse me while I go get her! (MORDECHAI *exits, fast, followed by* MAJOR-DOMO.)

HAMAN. Listen, sire, about that favor you owe me—

KING. Not so fast, Haman! First I want to see how

your plan works. And there had better be a real looker in the bunch!

ZARES. (*To* HAMAN.) *Now* you've done it, you numb-skull!

HAMAN. *I've* done it?! It was *your* idea that he should—!

ZARES. Quiet, the major-domo's coming back!

(*All turn as* MAJOR-DOMO *enters, stops just onstage, clears his throat while MUSIC intros, and then:*)

MAJOR-DOMO. (*Sings:*)
Your majesty, we have a cornucopia
Of maidens fair of form and sweet of voice.
Your empire from
India runs clear to Ethiopia,
So there's lots of them from which to make your
    choice!
Now, here they come . . .
    (*As each is named,* BEAUTY CONTESTANTS *enter,
    one from left, then one from right, criss-crossing
    stage until all form a line with* ESTHER *dead
    center, facing us.*)
Presenting Miss Abyssinia,
Illustration of the gentle desert joys!
And secondly, Miss Sardinia,
The embodiment of middle-eastern poise!
The third, Miss Thrace,
Is the archetype of grace!
And the fourth, Miss Phrygia's
Endowments are prodigious!
The fifth, Miss Ur—
Get a load of her!—
With her cap of fur so cute!

The sixth is Miss Macedonia!
(In all candor, Alexander wants her bad!)
The seventh is Miss Laconia!
(She's the sort to drive a mortal man quite mad!)
And Miss Sudan,
Number eight, is spic-and-span!
Number nine, Sumeria's
Contestant, is gregarious!
The tenth, Miss Crete,
On petite pink feet,
Is a sweet athlete, to boot!

Eleven's
Miss Jordan,
The sort you'd never want to shelve!
And you'll need
A warden
To guard Miss Carthage, number twelve!

Miss Cyprus, our number thirteen, you
Will observe has rather curvy overlays!
The fourteenth is called Miss Corinth, who
Can be fun in half-a-hundred diff'rent ways!
And fifteen is
Rather nifty Miss Cadiz,
And the sixteenth gal, we u—
Nderstand is called Miss Chaldea. . . .
    (ESTHER *enters timidly and takes her place,
    center, during:*)
This final dame has no claim to fame,
If it's all the same to you.
She says she's just plain Esther,
But I guess you'll like the view.
You may find a queen 'mid the seventeen
As with each you rendezvous . . .

So look 'em all over,
And call me when you're through!

(MAJOR-DOMO *exits, and* CONTESTANTS *all turn upstage
to face the* KING, *and drop down upon one knee,
heads bowed.*)

HAMAN. (*Anxiously.*) Well, your majesty, do you
see one you like, huh? If you don't find a bride in this
bunch, I'm sure there must be some more, someplace
around! Shall I go and see? I mean, if you're not really
turned on by any of these, I don't mind in the least
going all over the empire to try and find you a—
ZARES. (*Tugs him aside.*) Husband! Be silent! Can
you not see the king is thinking?!

(*All stand waiting—except the kneeling* CONTESTANTS,
of course—as the KING *strolls from center to left,
then all the way back to right, then finally back
to center, studying the semi-prostrated maidens;
then he nods, satisfied, and claps his hands, once;*
MAJOR-DOMO *hastens onstage and goes to him.*)

MAJOR-DOMO. Sire? Have you reached your de-
cision?
KING. I have.
HAMAN. (*Comes gingerly forward.*) You *do* like *one*
of them, don't you? I'd feel just terrible, if—
KING. Fear not, Haman. I have seen them all—and
I have chosen!
MAJOR-DOMO. And whom have you chosen, sire?
Who is to be the new queen of the Persian Empire—?
KING. Is it not obvious—? (*Sings:*)
Who's got the lips that put the roses to shame? . . .

Esther!
Who's got a figure that's the name of the game? . . .
Esther!
Who could make philanderers all vow to be true?
Who could charm the pictures off a sailor's tattoo?
Who's so gorgeous that they should arrest her? . . .
ALL BUT CONTESTANTS.
Esther, that's who!

(*During remainder of song,* KING *will take* ESTHER
*gently by the hand, bring her to her feet, lead her
to the smaller of the two thrones, seat her there,
signal the* MAJOR-DOMO *with a gesture,* MAJOR-
DOMO *will exit and return presently with a royal
crown similar to the* KING'S, *and—at the place
indicated—will place the crown upon her head.*)

KING.
Who stops the traffic at the chariot-race? . . . Esther!
EUNUCHS.
Who's got the eunuchs singing baritone-bass? . . .
Esther!
MORDECHAI.
Who can turn a heart into a hunk of debris?
MAJOR-DOMO.
Who can find a welcome-mat on ev'ry man's knee?
KING.
Who could keep the pupils all semester?
ALL BUT ESTHER.
Esther!
ESTHER.
That's me!
KING.
The day I met her—

ALL BUT ESTHER.

When they met . . .

KING.

I might have known—

ALL BUT ESTHER.

He might have known . . .

KING.

Some day I'd set her—

ALL BUT ESTHER.

Set her right there . . .

KING.

Upon the throne!

   (*Crowns her.*)

ESTHER.

With a crown of my own!

OTHERS.

Yeah!

KING.

Who cuddles closer than a chummy sardine?

CONTESTANTS.

Who is the scenery when she makes the scene?

ALL BUT ESTHER.

Who could never be a second-bester?

Esther, our Queen!

ESTHER.

Well, can you beat it!

ALL OTHERS.

Esther, our Queen!

ESTHER.

Oh, please repeat it!

ALL OTHERS.

Esther . . . our Queen!

KING. Well, now, let's see about getting the new queen some suitable garments, a staff of servants, her own personal chariot— (*He is strolling off as he speaks,*

trailed by MAJOR-DOMO *and* ALL OTHERS EXCEPT
ESTHER, MORDECHAI, HAMAN, ZARES *and* CONTEST-
ANTS.) a couple of dozen eunuchs, her name carven
beside mine upon the royal obelisk—oh, don't forget
to scrape off ex-Queen Vashti's— (*They are gone;*
HAMAN, *curious, approaches* MORDECHAI.)

HAMAN. Excuse me, but—I don't believe I know
you . . . ?

MORDECHAI. My name is Mordechai.

HAMAN. Are you a citizen of Susan?

MORDECHAI. Yes, I am.

HAMAN. Funny, you don't *look* Persian.

MORDECHAI. I am a Jew.

HAMAN. A Jew? I thought all you people were cap-
tives of the Babylonians.

MORDECHAI. Well, we were—but there aren't any
more Babylonians.

HAMAN. Oh, that's right. What ever happened to
them anyhow?

MORDECHAI. Don't you remember? . . . Daniel . . .
the handwriting on the wall . . . the death of Bel-
shazzar . . . the Babylonian kingdom divided between
the Medes and the Persians? Well, I'm with the group
that ended up with the Persians.

HAMAN. Of course! It all comes back to me, now!
You Jews are dangerous people to have around.

ZARES. You destroy from within!

MORDECHAI. It was God who destroyed the Babylonians.

HAMAN. God? Which God?

ZARES. After all, there are so many of them! (HAMAN
and ZARES *exit in the direction the* KING *took*.)

MORDECHAI. Esther—I think that, for the time being,
at least—you'd better not mention to anyone that
you're Jewish.

ESTHER. I'm not afraid of Haman.

MORDECHAI. He has great influence with the King—and there are a lot of Jews in this empire . . .

ESTHER. Naturally, I will do whatever you command me.

MORDECHAI. Good girl. Well, I guess I'd better be leaving, now.

ESTHER. I wish you'd stay on, at the palace.

MORDECHAI. Maybe someday—right now, I think for your own best interests, I should lie low. I don't like the idea of the King owing Haman a favor. I smell trouble.

ESTHER. As you wish. Here, let me escort you to the palace doors! (ESTHER *and* MORDECHAI *exit; the* CONTESTANTS *all sigh, look about at each other, and:*)

(MISS) ABYSSINIA. Well—you win a few, you lose a few.

CADIZ. I hate to think of the long boat-ride home!

SUMERIA. I'd gladly swap with you: I'm facing a thousand-mile journey by *camel!* (*All look up as* MAJOR-DOMO *enters.*)

MAJOR-DOMO. Ladies, good news!

THRACE. We could use some.

MAJOR-DOMO. None of you have to go home. The King has decided that, since you were all such good sports about losing, you can stay on here at the palace —as Queen Esther's handmaidens!

PHRYGIA. What's *third* prize?

MAJOR-DOMO. I beg your pardon—?

LACONIA. Don't mind her—she's only joking.

CORINTH. Actually, we're all quite honored.

MACEDONIA. What maiden *wouldn't* give her teeth to be in our shoes?!

CARTHAGE. (*After a pause.*) Don't all answer at once.

MAJOR-DOMO. Do I detect a note of discontent?

SARDINIA. What?

UR. Nonsense!

SUDAN. We're delighted the King selected us!

JORDAN. And it has nothing to do with the fact—

CRETE. —that to refuse a royal invitation is death!

CYPRUS. A slow, lingering death!

CHALDEA. The real reason we're pleased is because of the way we feel about Queen Esther, herself! (*MUSIC INTROS, and:*)

CONTESTANTS. (*Sing:*)

She's so lovely, we simply had to lose.

She's so charming, we'll never sing the blues.

No denying

She's quite electrifying.

She's so lovely . . .

(*Confidentially, to audience:*)

Let's hope she blows a fuse!

(*For* MAJOR-DOMO'S *ears:*)

She's so lovely, we never had a chance.

She's so charming, so just-right for romance.

Warm and willing,

And absolutely thrilling!

She's so lovely . . .

(*To audience:*)

Let's kick her in the pants!

(*To* MAJOR-DOMO:)

The king decrees her

The sweetest on this planet!

We'd love to squeeze her . . .

(*To audience:*)

Between two blocks of granite!

(*To* MAJOR-DOMO:)

She's so lovely! They're such a pretty pair!

She's so charming, with gorgeousness to spare!

(*Satisfied,* MAJOR-DOMO *exits, and they continue, now directly to audience:*)

Oh, what glee if
We got the chance to see if
She's so lovely . . .
Once we pulled out her hair!

She makes men smolder!
She's Persia's fav'rite daughter!
We'd love to hold her . . .
Ten minutes underwater!
   (*During remainder of song,* ESTHER *re-enters, re-acts, comes down and listens serenely to singers, who, of course, are not aware of her presence.*)
It's presumptuous to speak of her this way:
She's so scrumptious, *he*'d take our breath away!
She's so lovely,
They go so hand-in-glovely,
We wish we were above le—
Gality . . .
'Cause
When we got through
With Esther-Poo,
How lovely could she be?!
   ESTHER. (*Quietly.*) "Esther-Poo"?
   ABYSSINIA. Yipe!
   CARTHAGE. It's the Queen! (*All prostrate themselves.*)
   CRETE. (*Raises her head slightly to ask:*) Uh . . . how long were you standing there, majesty—?
   ESTHER. (*With dry amusement.*) About twenty-four bars.
   SUMERIA. All at once, that camel-ride doesn't seem so bad!
   ESTHER. (*Laughs.*) Ladies, ladies! Please get up.

(*When they hesitate:*) I mean it. Really. Come, now, on your feet. You have nothing to fear from me.

CADIZ. (*As they arise, still shaken with dread.*) But—majesty—if you heard what we were just saying . . . ?

ESTHER. Of course I heard. And I quite understand. I think I'd feel the same way, myself, if one of you had been the winner. (*As they sigh with relief and relax a bit:*) *However*—I don't think that sort of thing should continue. Do you?

ALL. (*Ad-lib various things like:*) Oh, no! . . . Of course not! . . . Never again! . . . Unh-uh! . . . No, your majesty!

ESTHER. Good, then the entire matter is forgotten. Now, follow me, ladies, while we see about getting you some suitably luxurious accommodations! (*All exit, with* LACONIA *and* CYPRUS *last.*)

LACONIA. You know something—I'm going to *like* working for *her!*

CYPRUS. Me, too! She could've had us rotating on a barbecue spit!

LACONIA. I guess the old saying is true: The bigger they are, the nicer they are!

CYPRUS. *Barbecue spits?!*

LACONIA. Come along, child, I'll spell it out for you in alphabet blocks.

CYPRUS. Who can *read?* (*They exit last, and* MORDECHAI *enters from opposite side, once again addressing us directly.*)

MORDECHAI. It was just a few days later, when the six-month-long celebration was at an end, that I happened to be in the throne room . . . (*Will move up and step partly behind the Queen's throne.*) Esther liked to have me around, for advice, for news of her people, sometimes just for friendly company, but she kept me out of sight behind her throne, so my humble robes wouldn't irritate the likes of Haman and Zares. Well, anyhow, I was waiting for court to convene, for the day's royal business, when all at once—

(BAGATHAN *and* THARES *enter.* MORDECHAI *moves back a bit out of view, and listens to them.*)

THARES. You sure you got the plan straight, now?

BAGATHAN. Of course I have. Tonight, when the King makes his way down that corridor to the Queen's bedroom, we jump him!

THARES. Lucky for us he always heads that way alone!

BAGATHAN. What do you expect? When a man joins his bride in the bedroom, he's hardly likely to bring along a drum-and-bugle corps!

THARES. Don't make me laugh—my back still aches from that flogging.

BAGATHAN. You'll have worse than a backache if we don't bring this off.

THARES. It's easy as pie. I hold his mouth, you tighten the bowstring around his neck. He'll be dead in two minutes.

BAGATHAN. For our sakes, he'd better be! Kings don't take kindly to assassins.

THARES. But they never say a *word* about *successful* assassins! (*Both chuckle, then look offstage.*) Hey, someone's coming! Let's clear out of here!

BAGATHAN. Right! (*They exit; then* KING *and* ESTHER *enter, opposite, and sit upon their respective thrones.*)

KING. Esther, I cannot begin to tell you what a happy man you've made me since becoming my bride.

ESTHER. You honor me, my lord. I am glad you find me pleasing.

MORDECHAI. Psst! Esther!

KING. Did you hear a hissing sound?

ESTHER. It might have been the wind, my lord. As winter nears, the palace grows drafty. (*He accepts this, and she leans sideways to whisper:*) Mordechai—is anything the matter?

MORDECHAI. Plenty! I have an urgent message for the King!

ESTHER. But *you* cannot address the King, Mordechai. Only his appointed officials, or other royalty, may do so.

MORDECHAI. That's what I'm counting on: *You're* royalty, now. Just relay my message to him!

KING. Esther? What are you doing?

ESTHER. I was—*pondering*, my lord. I have an urgent message for you, but I—I was uncertain just how I should phrase it.

KING. (*Smiles indulgently.*) Any words from your sweet lips are as honey in my ears. Proceed, in any manner you choose.

ESTHER. Thank you, my lord. . . .

KING. Well—?

ESTHER. (*Out front, hopefully awaiting further information.*) Well . . .

(*MUSIC INTROS; during song, all* MORDECHAI'S *words will be sung to* ESTHER, *and all the* KING'S *words to* ESTHER; ESTHER, *of course, will be singing first to one man, then to the other, as she acts as go-between.*)

MORDECHAI. (*Sings:*)
I bring you sad tidings—

ESTHER.
I bring you sad tidings—
KING.
And what are the tidings?
ESTHER.
Hold on, while I check! . . .
What tidings?
MORDECHAI.
Two eunuchs—
ESTHER.
Two eunuchs—
MORDECHAI.
Are plotting—
ESTHER.
Are plotting—
KING.
To what?
ESTHER.
What?
MORDECHAI.
To wring the king's neck!
ESTHER.
My lord, they will throttle you!
KING.
When?
ESTHER.
When?
MORDECHAI.
Say, "Not till you
Start down the hallway en route to your bed!"
ESTHER.
At bedtime.
KING. (*Not panic, just negation:*)
Oh, no!

ESTHER.

No.

MORDECHAI.

Then what?

ESTHER.

What will you do?

KING.

I'll kill them so quickly they'll wish they were dead!
But tell me, who are they?

ESTHER.

Who are they?

MORDECHAI.

Their names are Bagathan and Thares.

ESTHER.

Bagathan and—
Who?

MORDECHAI.

And Thares!

ESTHER.

And Thares!

KING.

Bagathan and Thares?
How sad, for I like them!

ESTHER.

But they don't like you!

KING.

No neck they'll be wringing.
I soon shall be stringing
Them up!

ESTHER.

They'll be swinging
Against the blue sky!

KING.

I thank you!

Esther.

Not me, sire!

King.

Then who?

Esther.

Thank the man who told *me!*

(*Draws* Mordechai *from behind throne.*)

King.

What's his name?

Esther.

Darling, meet Mordechai!

King. (*Clasps* Mordechai's *hand.*) A pleasure! You shall be rewarded! But first, I have a couple of eunuchs to take care of! (*Exits, calling:*) Guards! Guards!

Mordechai. (*When* King *is gone.*) He seems rather nice. I hope you're happy with him?

Esther. Oh, yes. But—I wish I could tell him I'm Jewish. I don't like keeping secrets from my husband.

Mordechai. Just a little while longer, Esther. Until I feel surer about Haman.

Esther. I shall obey. Now, if you'll excuse me, I have to see the royal chef about today's luncheon.

Mordechai. Come to think of it, I could use some lunch, myself. See you later! (*She waves and exits; he is about to exit, opposite, when* Haman *and* Zares *enter.*) Hail to thee, Haman.

Haman. Why do you not bow?

Mordechai. Bow?

Zares. Know you not that the gracious King, to do honor to my husband, has proclaimed that all shall do him honor throughout the empire, by the bowing of the head and the bending of the knee as he does pass?

Mordechai. I shall gladly bow my head, but I bend my knee to none but my God.

Haman. I can have you killed for this!

MORDECHAI. I had thought none but the King could order the taking of a life.

ZARES. Husband, I fear he is right!

HAMAN. I'm getting sick of this, Mordechai! And I don't like you hanging around my gate, either! If you do not bend the knee to me, you will set a bad example among the townspeople!

MORDECHAI. Your gate is on a public street. If I pause there to enjoy the sun, what is that to you?

HAMAN. Watch your tongue, Jew! With the power at my disposal, with my influence upon the King, I can have *all* the Jews destroyed!

MORDECHAI. Many a tyrant has said that before— and many will say as much hence—but the people God has chosen for his own will not be destroyed by godless men. I regret I have been the cause of your hatred for my people—but I do not fear the outcome of your wrath. Beware, lest your hatred, unfulfilled—like unto an arrow shot aloft toward a swift-soaring eagle, which, missing its mark, returns to sender—will rebound unto your own destruction! (*Exits with dignity.*)

ZARES. Husband—maybe you'd better cool off. After all, you have wealth, and power, and limitless luxury. Perhaps you should rest content.

HAMAN. Content? How can I be content? All that I have, all that I do, all that I am—is as nothing! Nothing, do you hear? Nor can I find contentment at all, so long as Mordechai will not accept my glory, nor bend to me as is my due!

ZARES. Is he then so painful to you?

HAMAN. I'll say he is! (*Sings:*)

He's the worm in my red apple, he's the puncture in
    my boat,

He's the gristle in my scrapple, he's the fishbone in my
    throat!

He's the sputter in my candle, he's the dandruff in my
    hair,
He's the pebble in my sandal, he's the sliver in my
    chair!

Why, why, Mordechai,
Must you make me sob and sigh?
Why, why can't you try just to be a nicer guy?
I would like to state: Mordechai's the guy I hate!
I can't concentrate while he's hanging round my gate!

He's the rip in my umbrella, of my party he's the
    death!
    ZARES.
You're the fly, he's citronella!
    HAMAN.
He's the garlic on my breath!
His mere presence can upset me!
    ZARES.
You're the roast beef, he's the knife!
    HAMAN.
Though he isn't out to get me, he is lousing up my
    life!
    BOTH.
Ev'rything we've got
Turns to rust and starts to rot
Till it goes to pot, just 'cause he is on that spot!
We must make him pay! At our gate he shall not stay!
There's no other way: Mordechai must die today!

    ZARES. Even so, husband, I fear the outcome of this.
Now that the King has proclaimed that all in the
empire must do you honor, he owes you a favor no
more!

    HAMAN. Ah, but what would he do to one who then
did *not* do me honor?!

ZARES. Most excellent husband, you have hit upon it! You have but to tell the King, and *he* shall destroy Mordechai *for* you!

HAMAN. Mordechai is no longer enough! The King shall destroy *all* the Jews! But, first things first—let us go, now, and have a gibbet built, from which we may merrily watch Mordechai choke away his life! (*They exit;* MORDECHAI *re-enters and addresses us.*)

MORDECHAI. Now, even with slave-labor, it took awhile to build that gibbet, so it was a few days later that the plot thickened like crazy . . . (*Gestures toward where* ESTHER *enters; as she seats herself upon the throne,* MORDECHAI *exits, and as soon as he is gone,* KING *enters and approaches* ESTHER.)

KING. My Queen, I fear I have been terribly remiss in an important matter!

ESTHER. What matter is that, my lord?

KING. So taken up have I been by the affairs of state that in my deep preoccupation I have never gotten around to rewarding that man who apprised me of the treason afoot against me—what was his name?

ESTHER. "Mordechai," my lord.

KING. Ah, yes, of course! But—what sort of reward would be suitable?

ESTHER. Well, my lord, perhaps— (*Pauses as* HAMAN *enters.*)

HAMAN. Your majesty, I would like to make a request of you . . .

KING. And so you shall, beloved Haman—but first, I have something that *I* must ask of *you!*

HAMAN. Of course, sire. Anything, sire!

KING. I merely require the answer to a question. There is a man in this kingdom—a good man—a loyal man—a man I do dearly love—I need not tell you his name—

HAMAN. (*Thinking it is himself.*) Oh, no, sire! I can practically guess it!

KING. This man has been of inestimable service to me, Haman—so much so that I find myself hard-pressed to think of a suitable reward!

HAMAN. You mean—you wish me to name my *own* re—? That is, my own idea of the reward that should go to this man so worthy of great honor?!

KING. Yes! You are a man who appreciates the finer things in life! Who else could give me a truer answer on such a subject?

HAMAN. Who else, indeed! Oh, there are so many things I—that is, he—that is, I think that he should have!

KING. Then name them, good Haman. If you were the King, and that man were standing here before the throne, where you stand right now, how would you show your gratitude and generosity to him?

HAMAN. (*Almost delirious with delight.*) Oh, your majesty, how *wouldn't* I show it! (*Sings:*)
I'd give him gold! I'd give him jade!
I'd give him horses and a ride in a parade!
I'd give him oxen roasting on the fire
To music by a classy choir,
And any little heart's desire he'd say!

I'd give him wine! I'd give him milk!
I'd give him honey, lots of money, suits of silk!
I'd give him statues throughout all the town,
Perhaps a tiny jeweled crown,
And just a humble palace down the way!

I'd give him dancing-girls equipped with
Entrancing curls and eyes,

And ev'ry goblet that he sipped with
His name would advertise!

I'd give him joy! I'd give him song!
I'd give him tender-loving-splendor all day long!
I'd give him ev'rything the heart can hunger for . . .
And then I'd subsequently give him plenty more!
    (*Philosophically:*)
It has often crossed my mind that life is all too fast
And fleeting,
And one's chances to be kind are all too few.
Man must die, but must he starve when he could die
    from
Over-eating?
So, when being nice to others, here's exactly what I'd
    do . . .
    (*Up-tempo again, dancing as he sings:*)
I'd hold his hand! I'd pour his tea!
I'd give him winning tickets for a lottery!
And I would try to keep him satisfied
With nightingales at eventide
And summers in the sun beside the sea!

I'd give him drapes, and silver spoons,
I'd give him manicures, massages, macaroons!
I'd give him golden bullion brick-on-brick,
A ruby-handled walking-stick,
And in a war I'd give him victory!

His fav'rite dog would get a flea-cap,
His frog would wear a bell,
And if he fell and skinned his kneecap,
I'd kiss and make it well!

I'd comb his beard! I'd give him gum!
I'd give him candy full of brandy laced with rum!

I'd give him
Sandalwood and teak
And cozy pats upon the cheek,
A hundred emeralds to wear,
A nest of peacocks in his hair,
Plus a performing bear, and parrots by the score . . .
And then I'd subsequently give him plenty more!
   (*Ends before throne on one knee á la Jolson, and
   says:*) Did I forget anything?

ESTHER. The kitchen sink.

HAMAN. (*To* KING:) And one of those!

KING. Marvelous, Haman! A brilliant list! But do
you not wish to know the name of the man upon whom
all these gifts will be bestowed?

HAMAN. (*Comes to his feet, eagerly.*) Yes, sire! Of
course, sire! Who is it, sire?

KING. His name is Mordechai.

HAMAN. (*It hasn't registered; thinks it's himself as
he drops to his knees and clutches the* KING'S *hand.*)
And let me say, I'll never stop being grateful that you
were so—so—! . . . *Who* did you say—?

KING. Mordechai. A middle-aged man, about so tall,
who's usually to be found standing out near—

HAMAN. (*Dully.*) Out near my gate. Check.

KING. But Haman—I had nearly forgotten—what
was it you wished to see me about?

HAMAN. (*Glumly, smiling weakly, backing off.*) It
. . . it will keep . . . sire. And now—if you'll excuse
me—I have a kind of—headache . . . ! (*Exits.*)

KING. How exceedingly strange he looked. Was it
something I said?

ESTHER. He was—probably overcome by our magnif-
icent generosity, my lord.

KING. Yes. Yes, that was probably it. Well—
(*Rises.*) That's enough royal business for today. Shall
we take a stroll in the royal gardens, my dear?

ESTHER. (*Sees* MORDECHAI *peek in and beckon to her.*) Uh . . . Why don't you go on ahead, my lord? I shall join you there in a moment or so . . .

KING. Very well, my dear. Don't be long, now! (*Starts off, then stops.*) Oh, drat! I forgot! I'm supposed to meet with my ministers on the fiscal situation —distribution of winter wheat to the poor—repaving the highways—it's a bore, but I cannot put it off.

ESTHER. The gardens will still be there for us later, my lord.

KING. I hope you're right. We got them from the Babylonians, you know, and my engineers can't quite get the *hang* of them. Ah well! (*Exits;* MORDECHAI *approaches* ESTHER *at once.*)

MORDECHAI. Dreadful news, Esther! Simply dreadful!

ESTHER. What, has Haman refused to give you the reward he dreamed up for you?

MORDECHAI. What? Oh, that! No, I'm afraid I had to refuse those gifts, under the circumstances.

ESTHER. What circumstances?

MORDECHAI. Haman is readying the army, and messengers to the other armies throughout the empire —he plans to have every last Jew slaughtered!

ESTHER. But how can he? Without the King's permission—?

MORDECHAI. You forget his popularity with the King. He plans to tell him that the Jews will not kneel to him, that they will not worship the King himself! Once this is done, the King will surely give his consent!

ESTHER. This shall not happen! It must not! Go, at once, and tell my eunuchs I would have Haman join myself and the King tonight, at dinner!

MORDECHAI. He's ready to kill your people, and you invite him to dinner?

ESTHER. I have a plan. Remember, Mordechai, I have a certain popularity with the King, myself.

MORDECHAI. Yes, but you cannot invite Haman to dinner without the King knowing about it, first.

ESTHER. Have no fear. I shall go to the King right now, and tell him of the planned invitation.

MORDECHAI. Now? But the King is closeted with his ministers! No one dare approach him unless he send for him! It could mean your death!

ESTHER. (*Simply.*) Then I shall be the first of my people to perish. If this slaughter comes to be, I should not have lasted long, anyhow.

MORDECHAI. Esther—you are the bravest woman I have ever known.

ESTHER. No. Not brave. Just—obedient to my God. When the choice arises, between my God and my life —I know where duty lies. Now go! (*As he hurries out.*) And send my handmaidens, with my most elegant finery!

MORDECHAI. It shall be done!

ESTHER. (*When he has gone.*) Brave! Oh, how I wish I were! (*Heavenward:*) Oh, sweet God—help me in my enterprise—counsel me in my words— direct my footsteps upon the path that shall lead me to this salvation of my people. I know that, with You beside me, I cannot fail—but it's so hard not to be afraid . . . ! (HANDMAIDENS *enter, bearing various items.*)

HANDMAIDEN. You summoned us, my Queen?

ESTHER. Yes! Hasten to make me ready!

HANDMAIDEN # 2. For what, my Queen?

ESTHER. I must approach the King in his council-chambers, now.

HANDMAIDEN # 3. Has the King sent for you, my
Queen?

ESTHER. If he had, I wouldn't be going to all this
trouble, would I?! (*As they sigh in sympathy, she will
sing, and make her selection of items as they come
up:*)
'Tis death to come unsummoned to the King,
And to my life I'd rather like to cling.
Perhaps if I put on another ring,
The King I might distract
From cutting short my act . . . !

More perfume to remind him I'm his wife.
Some bangles tinkling out an ode to life.
An extra veil might tangle up his knife
The while I tell him why
I happened to drop by!
    HANDMAIDENS.
Approaching in this manner, it's an awful handicap to
Know his royal temper's apt to
Cause a scene!
    ESTHER.
Yet duty bids me tell him that his royal proclamation
May entail the liquidation
Of the Queen!

I'm sure that I'm the apple of his eye—
    HANDMAIDENS.
But apples often end up in a pie!
    ESTHER.
Yet if I wait, my people all will die!
    ESTHER and HANDMAIDENS.
How can I/you beguile his royal majesty . . .
    ESTHER.
When I cannot send him till he sends for me?! (*Sighs,
looks her attire over; then:*) Well—how do I look?

HANDMAIDEN # 4. My Queen, if you don't turn him on, at first sight—*he's* the one who's *dead!*

ESTHER. Thank you, all of you. Well—here goes nothing! (*She exits timidly but regally,* HANDMAIDENS *exit opposite, and* MORDECHAI *enters and addresses us:*)

MORDECHAI. As you might have guessed—since I'm here to tell this story—Esther not only got in to see the King, he called the entire meeting off, and they had their walk in the garden. And while they did, of course, she told him about Haman coming to dinner, and the King said fine, and then, when they'd finished their after-dinner coffee—coffee *came* to us from the Persians, you know—well, let me *show* you how things came out. . . . (MORDECHAI *secretes himself behind Queen's throne, and then* ESTHER *and* HAMAN *stroll in.*)

HAMAN. Majesty, that dinner was a marvel! And I was so pleased to learn that the King's invitation came at your suggestion! You know, I haven't told the King yet—but I'm planning a bit of sport that you and he might find amusing!

ESTHER. Does it have something to do with that gibbet you have had built just outside the palace walls?

HAMAN. Oh, you noticed!

ESTHER. Well, it *is* forty-five cubits high.

HAMAN. Fifty! But yes, that is a part of it. You remember that man the King asked me to honor—?

ESTHER. Mordechai? Yes, I remember him well.

HAMAN. Well, when I get through telling the King about him—*Mordechai* is going to be dangling from that gibbet!

ESTHER. What a pity! And me with no mourning dress to wear!

HAMAN. Mourning? Why would you mourn Mordechai?

ESTHER. (*Casually.*) Why would I not? After all, he *is* my *father!*

HAMAN. (*Shocked.*) He? Who he? You mean *him?* Mordechai? *The* Mordechai? Your *father?*

ESTHER. Actually, he's not my *real* father.

HAMAN. Oh, that's good!

ESTHER. But I love him as much as if he were.

HAMAN. Oh, that's bad!

ESTHER. But, of course, you have great popularity with the King.

HAMAN. Oh, good!

ESTHER. But mine's even greater.

HAMAN. Oh, bad!

ESTHER. So, when I *tell* the King you have plotted against the life of my father—the man, who, by the way, just recently saved the King's *life*—welllll—?!

HAMAN. (*Clutches at her, frantically.*) Wait, majesty! Listen! So I made a little *mistake*—! . . . Whoops!

(*Tripping on the edge of the dais,* HAMAN *sits with a thud, and* ESTHER—*whose arm he still holds— comes tumbling back down onto his lap; and as they sit there startled, almost in an embrace, the* KING *enters.*)

KING. Well, well, what have we here? I give you honor, I give you power, I give you dinner, even, and how do you repay me? By trying to make out with the Queen!

HAMAN. (*To* ESTHER, *desperately.*) *Say* something!

ESTHER. Such as?

MORDECHAI. (*Steps from behind throne.*) If you need a witness, I saw the whole thing!

HAMAN. Now, wait, hold it just a minute! (*Sings:*)
Majesty!
Things aren't this bad! You see,
I merely stumbled—
Then all at once we tumbled
Into a compromising
Kind of mess
That could stop your kindliness!
  KING.
That's for sure!
  HAMAN.
If you'll just listen, we can soon clear it up!
  KING.
Well, this I've got to hear!
  HAMAN. (*Assisting* ESTHER *to her feet, getting up himself.*)
Tell him, sweet Queen, why he found this naughty
    scene!
  ESTHER.
Why, my dear Haman, whatever do you mean?
  MORDECHAI.
Just tell what's true!
  HAMAN.
Please back me!
  QUEEN.
He came here to
Attack me!
  KING.
What?!
  ESTHER and MORDECHAI.
We don't mean
The obscene way!
  KING.
Which way do you mean?
  HAMAN.
I hope there's another!

ESTHER.

He came here tonight with the news—
  KING.

What news did he bring in?
  ESTHER.

That he planned to slaughter the Jews!
  HAMAN.

So far, so good! Continue!
  MORDECHAI.

You see, he was hoping to beg this boon—
  KING. (*Unconvinced.*)

Oh, sure!
  ESTHER.

Not knowing the trouble that he would soon
Endure!
  HAMAN.

That's the fact of it!
  MORDECHAI.

It seemed that his dream would come true—
  KING.

Thanks to his wheeler-dealing—
  ESTHER.

But there's something he never knew—
  HAMAN.

I've got this sinking feeling . . .
  MORDECHAI.

While he did not mean
To endanger your Queen—
  ESTHER.

Still, he did!
  MORDECHAI.

For, this kid—
  ESTHER and MORDECHAI.

Is a Jew!

KING.

Ah, so?

HAMAN.

Oh, no!

KING. Let me see if I have this straight—Haman planned to use my armies to wipe out the Jewish people—

ESTHER. Starting with Mordechai, the man who saved your life—

MORDECHAI. On that fifty-cubit gibbet he just built outside the wall.

HAMAN. (*Hopelessly.*) Forty-five.

KING. And in the course of such a slaughter, for which I would first have to give my royal approval—

ESTHER. Your Queen would be slaughtered with the rest—

MORDECHAI. Since she could hardly wish to live, with all her people destroyed.

HAMAN. I don't blame her. You know, now that I've thought this thing over—I'd just like to say— (*Almost a sob.*) I'm sorry!

KING. I have thought it over, too. Mordechai, go and tell my army it is my decree that they disband at once, and any man who harms a Jew will answer to me!

MORDECHAI. (*Starts out.*) Yes, sire! At once, sire! (*Pauses.*) Oh, shall I have them tear down that gibbet, too?

KING. No. Not yet. I think we may shortly be putting it to use. (*Winks.*)

MORDECHAI. Gotcha! (*Winks back, exits.*)

KING. Well, Haman old buddy, I'm afraid it is my unpleasant duty to tell you that—

HAMAN. Wait! (*Sings:*)

Good King, before you go too far, re—
Mind yourself I said I'm sorry!
   KING.
Yes, of course, that's what you said,
And I shall let you keep your head!
     (HAMAN *smiles in relief.*)
But here is why I've spared your neck
And do not choose to chop it:
     (HAMAN'S *smile starts to slip.*)
A noose would slip right off your throat
Without a head to stop it!
   HAMAN. (*Very glum.*)
Oh gosh! Oh gee!
Oh, woe is me!
Oh, curse my indiscretions!
Farewell to joy!
Oh nuts! Oh boy! . . .
And similar expressions.
   ESTHER.
Your song is sung,
The trap is sprung,
The iron door has clanged.
   KING.
There's but one thing
That I, as king,
Can do—!
   HAMAN.
Well, I'll be hanged!
   ESTHER.
You planned your grim invasion
Upon the wrong persuasion.
   KING.
I'll bet right now that you wish
You'd known the Queen was Jewish!

HAMAN.

Oh, such a life!

KING.

It soon will cease.

HAMAN.

I'm on the skids!

ESTHER. (*To* KING:)

Don't spare the grease!

HAMAN.

What of my wife?

ESTHER.

She goes with you.

HAMAN.

And my ten kids?

KING.

We'll hang them too.

ESTHER and KING.

There's no escaping justice, after all,

So why debate? You can't fight city hall!

HAMAN.

Much less a monarch!

ESTHER and KING.

So, Haman, you are riding for a fall!

HAMAN.

From fifty cubits!

ESTHER and KING.

That old handwriting's back upon the wall!

KING. Guards! (*Two* GUARDS *enter*.) Take Haman away, get some more guards, go over to his house, get his wife, and his ten kids, and then—well—see how long it takes you to get them all strung up on that new gibbet outside the wall!

GUARDS. Yes, sire! At once, sire!

HAMAN. (*As they lead him off*.) Hey—listen—wait—checks, fellas—I got an idea—! (*The moment they are*

gone, Mordechai, Major-Domo, *and* Everybody Else
in the show except Haman *and* Zares *enter.*)

Mordechai. The army has been disbanded!

Handmaidens. And the Jewish people are cheering
in the streets!

Courtiers. And everybody in Susan is shouting the
Queen's name!

Nobles. What has she done? What's going on?

Major-Domo. I suspect you'll read all about it, soon
enough . . .

Mordechai. Because this is one for the history
books!

(*MUSIC INTROS, the* King *leads* Esther *to the
throne, seats her there,* Everybody Else *gathers
around, and:*)

King. (*Sings:*)
Now that it's over—
　　Others.
It's all done—
　　King.
It's plain to see—
　　Others.
Oh, yessiree—
　　King.
We'll be in clover—
　　Others.
Won't it be fun?!
　　King.
Eternally!
　　　　(*Kneels before* Esther.)
　　Esther.
With the King at my knee!

OTHERS.
Whee!

Whose future twinkles like the e-ven-ing star?
Who starts our hearts a-beating eight-to-the-bar?
Who is the greatest, heaven rest her?
Esther, by far!
ESTHER.
Oh, gosh, oh, golly!
OTHERS.
Esther, by far!
MORDECHAI. (*Right out front, to us:*)
What a finale!
ALL.
Esther, by far! . . .
Oh, yes, you are!

CURTAIN

The Plotters of Cabbage Patch Corner
Musical Play for Children
DAVID WOOD

6 male, 4 female
Audience participation. One basic setting.

The insects live in a busy world in the garden. Their existence, however, is always overshadowed by the humans—the Big Ones. Infuriated by constant "spraying" the unattractive Slug, Greenfly and Maggot call for rebellion, strikes, ruination of the garden. The others oppose this and war is declared. Fortune swings one way and the other in a series of bitter campaigns. The garden goes to ruin, and the Big Ones decide to build a garage on it. This brings the insects to their senses. They combine to restore the garden to its original beauty and thus preserve their home.

(ROYALTY, $25-$20)

The Ant and the Grasshopper
(Children's Play) Fantasy
ROB DEARBORN

9 characters (1 clearly female,
the others can be either male or female)

The classic tale updated with contemporary language and themes understood by today's children—and adults. An uptight, super-industrious ant has just opened a new branch ant-hole when an irresponsible, "hippytype" grasshopper moves in right next door. Ant resists Grasshopper's offers to join him and his friends, Caterpillar and Ladybug in play—in fact he says play is a bad word. For his diligence Ant is promoted by autocratic, imperious Queen Ant. With his two assistants Ant prepares for the coming winter. Grasshopper, naturally, doesn't believe in winter or any of the gloomy warnings of Ant and even the attacks of hungry Spider fails to daunt his optimism. But winter does come, and both Grasshopper, who has no food or shelter, and Ant, who has no friends and has never had any fun, discover at last that there is more to life than they thought.

(ROYALTY, $15)